TEACHING STUDENTS TO SELF-ASSESS

How do I help students reflect and grow as learners?

Starr
SACKSTEIN

 Alexandria, VA USA

Website: www.ascd.org   www.ascdarias.org
E-mail: books@ascd.org

Printed in the United States of America. Cover art © 2015 by ASCD. ASCD publications present a variety of viewpoints. The views expressed or implied in this book should not be interpreted as official positions of the Association.

ASCD LEARN TEACH LEAD® and ASCD ARIAS™ are trademarks owned by ASCD and may not be used without permission. All other referenced trademarks are the property of their respective owners.

PAPERBACK ISBN: 978-1-4166-2153-9   ASCD product #SF116025

Also available as an e-book (see Books in Print for the Isbns).

Library of Congress Cataloging-in-Publication Data
Names: Sackstein, Starr.
Title: Teaching students to self-assess : how do I help students reflect and grow as learners? / Starr Sackstein.
Description: Alexandria, Virginia : ASCD, [2015] | Includes bibliographical references.
Identifiers: LCCN 2015032991 | ISBN 9781416621539 (pbk. : alk. paper)
Subjects: LCSH: Students—Self-rating of—United States. | Educational tests and measurements—United States. | Reflective teaching—United States.
Classification: LCC LB3051 .S226 2015 | DDC 371.26—dc23 LC record available at http://lccn.loc.gov/2015032991

21 20 19 18 17 16 15   1 2 3 4 5 6 7 8 9 10 11 12

TEACHING STUDENTS TO SELF-ASSESS

How do I help students reflect and grow as learners?

Introduction

Education in the 21st century sometimes seems to be in a new language that has yet to be decoded. The traditional one-size-fits-all method of transmitting knowledge to passive students is no longer adequate. Today, learning is interactive and ever-changing, like our students. With information available in every corner of the world, students no longer rely on a single person to convey content. Instead, they need a guide to help them interpret the facts and the thoughts that they uncover. This new facilitative role of the educator enables students to go beyond what they already know and seek out knowledge that will help them develop and innovate.

To help students grow, we must teach them to develop the skill of metacognition—that is, to become aware of their own thought processes. If we teach students to know themselves well, they can ask the right questions and garner the help they need to become successful in every situation.

Reflection is an essential tool that enables students to decode what they know and what challenges them—and, most important, to distinguish between the two. Teaching reflection can help students decipher their own learning needs and elicit evidence from their own work to support their growth.

But giving students time to think about what they learned isn't enough; deep reflection and self-analysis are not innate skills. Students must be taught how to consider their work intelligently against standards to be able to show mastery and set goals for developing themselves as learners.

Teachers can use differentiation and scaffolding to help students go beyond simple regurgitation of words and facts to engage in deep, thought-provoking discourse about progress. Using a variety of written and spoken means, students can discuss what it is they know without taking tests or being told by a teacher. Providing students with examples of mastery, a clear understanding of expectations and standards, and multiple opportunities to explore content will enable them to grow into mindful, receptive learners, ready to explore the 21st century world.

Reading this book, you will learn

- What reflection is.
- How to teach reflection.
- When to use reflection.
- How to empower students to take charge of their own learning and assessment.

What Is Reflection and Why Should We Teach It?

A few years ago, I decided that it was time to dive deeply and honestly into my own practice. After 10 years of teaching, observation notes and student feedback weren't enough to push me to the next level, so I took on National Board Certification.

I got my first taste of the task's enormity when the "welcome box" arrived in the mail. It felt like hello in 12 languages I didn't speak. Undaunted, I began the arduous journey. Commencing with 112 pages of standards that defined what reflective teachers do, I eagerly made connections to my own practice, scrawling my annotations on the pages like graffiti.

It soon became evident that content knowledge was only a small percentage of the expectation. I'd need to scrutinize my practice over the course of a year, gathering materials from students, filming my classes, and meticulously examining the choices I made to foster students' learning. I was required to study my feedback to students and the resulting student growth, analyze both whole-class and small-group discussion, and evaluate community outreach and involvement. Watching the footage of my class discussions and group work, like a coach prepping for big game, I analyzed my delivery, questions, wait time, and even vocal intonation. The data I gathered on myself were invaluable and led me to make crucial changes to my practice and my behavior in the classroom.

Since achieving National Board Certification, reflection has become an integral part of my practice and my evolution as an educator. With a critical eye, I explore what works and what needs work, and I find solutions to help me continue to grow and keep up with the changing educational landscape.

Because of the incredible effect that reflection has had on my practice, I was eager to teach this tool to my students.

During the certification process, I began to connect the process of analyzing my own performance against teaching standards to what my students needed. How could I help students examine the choices they made as learners? How could helping them understand the skill expectations of a lesson better prepare them for success?

What Reflection Looks Like in the Classroom

Many of us think about stuff after it happens. The difference between reflection and just thinking about something, however, is *intention*. Let's examine what reflection looks like in the classroom. Teachers who incorporate student reflection effectively

- **Explicitly teach students what reflection is and allow them to practice during class time.** Effective teachers give students feedback on their reflections: what are students doing well? What could they do better? They highlight particular portions of students' reflections and offer strategies or ask probing questions to help them add depth—for example, "You clearly understood the information, but I'm not sure you were able to connect the content to the skills. Which standards did you address in this assignment, and how can you show your growth?"

- **Teach students to question everything.** Teachers who use reflection effectively help students understand how reflection engages them in their own thinking and learning processes and teach them that learning is active, not something that happens to them.

- **Avoid treating reflection as an add-on.** Instead, they teach reflection as a necessary, inextricable part of what is already happening in class.
- **Make reflection more about actual learning than about how much students liked the content or learning activity.** Effective teachers make expectations clear so that students have a baseline to assess their learning against and are able to discuss their learning in terms of the standards being taught.
- **Differentiate how students reflect.** Just as there is no single type of student, there is no one right way to do reflection. Teachers who effectively use reflection give students the freedom to choose how they reflect, whether in writing, through video, or in face-to-face conferences.
- **Ask students to share their reflections with others.** For example, teachers may have students maintain a reflection blog throughout the school year. Students can use a variety of tools to support their style of reflection, including social media websites or applications like Twitter, Blogger, WordPress, Voxer, and Instagram. These new techniques help teachers connect students' learning to the larger world outside school.
- **Model reflection.** Effective teachers model reflection often and share their process and insights with their students. I myself maintain two blogs in which I tackle issues that arise daily and share my experiences with others, encouraging dialogue. I often participate in Twitter chats with a rigorous community of

professionals that push me to consider my beliefs as an educator and validate my practices. Effective teachers also model continual growth after the reflection, putting into action what they've learned from the reflection process.

Benefits of Reflection

After every project my students complete, I eagerly read their reflections, seeking ways to improve their collective experience. My students have become adept at weaving their thoughts and experiences into evidence-based written pieces that explore learning and standards and honestly reflect the work they have done.

Tip: Always read students' reflections before reading their work. Doing so will help you focus your read of their work and provide specific feedback on what they are working on. This also ensures that you won't view their work through your own agenda.

It wasn't always this way—and if you're just beginning to use reflection as a learning tool, it may not be this way at first for you, either. When we first start reflecting, it can feel like a burden. If students don't understand why they are doing it, then it will seem superfluous to them. Thus, it is crucial to communicate to students *why* we reflect. They need to understand the value of reflection as it pertains to both their lives and their learning.

Once everyone begins reaping its benefits, it's easy to recognize that reflection is an important part of the learning process and essential to our overall growth. By developing metacognitive awareness, students can clearly understand and articulate what they know and can do and where they need to ask for help. Being able to identify one's own areas of strength and need is an essential life skill.

As teachers, we must make this point clear to our students, and we must value what they share with us in their reflections. Reflection is an opportunity for us to share a moment with each student and get inside his or her head, in the process deepening our relationship with that student. The insights we gather provide valuable context that we can apply in our practice. With a greater understanding of our students' needs, we are able to tailor our instruction and teach more effectively.

Since I started using reflection with my students, I've witnessed profound growth in their ability to discuss their learning. They understand themselves as learners and often develop strategies for working to their own strengths and weaknesses. They are capable of asking for help in ways they couldn't before, making them advocates for their own learning.

In that vein, I'll let students explain the benefits of reflection in their own words. The following quotation comes from a conversation I had with one of my seniors:

> Although I found reflections to be kind of a hassle in the beginning of the year, now I really appreciate taking the time to sit and write them. It allows

me to look back on the process of actually planning and writing my assignments as well as being able to identify the skills I actually learned and took away from the project. Reflections make me think about the challenges I faced and teach me how to approach similar problems in other situations.

Another senior explained how reflection helps her grow:

Reflecting on our learning helps us focus on what we need to work on in the future. If I write in my reflection that I am having troubles writing transitional phrases in my essays, I would know that in the next essay this is something specific that I want to review and work on. It helps the students and the teachers that read the reflections narrow into what should be taught or reviewed for the next assignment.

Reflection Questions:

1. Do you currently use reflection in your own learning? What does it look like?

2. How can making reflection a part of your students' learning enhance your ability to help them grow as learners and people?

3. How can reflection deepen teacher-student relationships and a person's relationship with him- or herself? How can reflection enhance a person's ability to learn?

Getting Started with Reflection

Goals are the necessary starting point to the learning process: all learning begins with setting the final objective. Thus, before students can reflect, they need to come up with learning goals—a process that is easier said than done. This section addresses how teachers can help students set reasonable goals and adjust their instruction based on the outcomes of those goals.

Helping Students Create Actionable Goals

How many times have you asked students to set learning goals, only to see statements like "I want to do better" and "I will complete all my work"? If your answer is "Too many times to count," then it's time to explicitly teach students what an actionable goal is and how to set one.

A major reason students get away with vague goals is that teachers aren't using goal setting as an authentic learning tool. Many teachers are accustomed to making the real choices for students, whether the goal is graduating or just passing the unit test. Instead of encouraging students to create focused, self-directed goals, they use goal setting as a way to fill time or to grant students a superficial sense of empowerment.

We need to reframe goal setting so that students understand how important goals are to the learning process and recognize that vague or unattainable goals will not help them succeed. Then we can guide them in creating their own robust learning goals. If goals are the front line in producing growth, then kids need to know why setting actionable long-term and short-term goals is essential to their success.

Figure 1 encapsulates the goal-setting process for students.

FIGURE 1: **A Guide to Setting Achievable Short-Term Goals**

What do I want to accomplish in the big picture?

Ask yourself

• What do I need to do to accomplish this goal?

• What smaller goals can I set that will help me achieve this goal?

• What is my timeline for achieving this goal?

• What specific steps will I take to accomplish this goal? (Break the goal down into a list of smaller steps.)

• How will I be held accountable for each of these steps?

• What happens if I don't reach my goals?

• How do these goals help me meet standards?

Here's how you can break down the steps and guide students in creating their own goals:

1. Have students write a list of long-term goals they would like to set for themselves. "Long-term" could be the span of a marking period or the length of one school year—no longer, or the goals will be too difficult to measure and thus lose their meaning.

2. Ask students to select one of these long-term goals to break down into several short-term goals.

3. Have students work in pairs to ask clarifying questions about the long-term goals they selected and tease out the finer points. For example, let's say a student's selected goal is "I'd like to do better in class." His or her partner may ask, "When you say you want to do better in class, what do you mean? Better at what, and in what way?" Using these prompts adds depth and dimension to the goals. The revised goal might be "I'd like to develop context in my writing to show a better understanding of the subject matter I'm writing about. This will meet the standards for development and help improve my writing." The more details students provide up front, the easier it will be for them to track their progress.

4. Now students are ready to come up with their short-term goals—no more than five, since they need to be manageable. Remind students to think in terms of the standards and their progress toward those standards. Which areas do they need to work on, according to such measures as class conferences, report cards, feedback on assignments, and short discussions during class? If your school doesn't

have standards, consider the overarching learning targets or expected outcomes.

5. Have students create a timeline with specific dates for accomplishing their short-term goals. They should make sure that the goals are attainable; there is nothing worse than setting a goal that can't possibly be met. This isn't to say we shouldn't encourage students to think big, but we also want them to experience success, so even word choice is important. Some examples of short-term goals that could emerge from the long-term goal above include improving introductory context while writing essays, generating seamless transitions in analysis papers, and contributing text-based thoughts in class conversation.

Once students have decided on a long-term goal and short-term goals and developed a timeline for reaching them, they can check tasks off their list as they accomplish them. It is extremely motivating for students to see their progress in real time. Setting specific due dates for goals raises the stakes and adds a gentle pressure to complete those goals on time. When students have set a goal for themselves, they are more invested in reaching it. For this reason, it is important for teachers not to take over and just assign students some goals. When we set students' goals for them, they are less effective and less likely to be met.

Tip: Allow students to be the master of their goals. Although there are overarching skills and content that all students must master by the end of a lesson or class, each student should be empowered to set the order and pace of his or her learning.

Make sure to emphasize that specificity is key to a goal's success, so students need to clearly articulate their goals and develop detailed plans to meet them. A goal without an action plan is just an empty statement. Have students clearly designate end points and intermediary checkpoints to facilitate continual reflection on their progress. When students are working on a major project, rather than just listing the big benchmarks, require students to check in after every step. For example, for a history research paper, the teacher should review each student's working thesis and check the student's research for appropriateness at the relevant stages in the process. Students can also work with peers to ensure that they're on the right track.

Finally, one of the best ways to show students that goal setting is a priority in your classroom is to share your own goals with them, along with the struggles you face while trying to achieve them. You'll not only model the process in an authentic way but also demonstrate that struggle can build perseverance, an essential life skill.

Adjusting Instruction Based on Student Goals and Reflection

We have explored how we can help students set learning goals and reflect on their progress toward those goals at designated checkpoints. How can we take the next step and use students' reflections to inform our teaching?

Although all students are striving for the same overarching learning objectives or standards, they come to them at different paces and through different avenues. Thus, if the true purpose of learning is mastery, we must figure out a way to tailor our instruction for every student. As a first step, whenever possible, incorporate individual student goals into the intended outcomes you develop for each student. Taking into consideration the goals students have set for their own learning will increase their level of buy-in and engagement.

Under no circumstances should teachers stand before their classes and lecture for entire periods. Most classes include anywhere from 20 to 34 students, so teachers must hold varying expectations and provide an array of activities to suit students' diverse needs. This may seem overwhelming, but this is where reflection comes in handy: students' ability to identify their challenges and ask pointed questions lightens our workload. Although it's nearly impossible to meet individually with every student every day, we *can* check in regularly and keep close tabs on all our students' learning. By reflecting on their progress toward their learning goals at multiple points during the learning process, students give us needed feedback and direct their own learning. As we help students become more self-aware, the directions they provide through their reflection generate an ongoing loop of learning that adjusts the scope, pace, and method of instruction as needed.

You can quickly ascertain where the class stands through exit tickets via Google Forms—a simple, streamlined way of gathering information—or short end-of-class reflections, intervening when necessary. If a majority of students aren't grasping key concepts or moving toward proficiency, it would be silly to move ahead. If the first lesson didn't do the trick, you may need to adjust your learning expectations and try something different the next day.

Most of the time, however, some students will get it and be ready to move on while others need to linger on the content a bit longer. In such cases, you can offer remediation outside class (e.g., during lunch), set up learning stations in class the next day, work with students one-on-one for remediation or acceleration, or recruit students who have mastered the content to mentor their classmates who need additional support or practice. If computers or tablets are available, consider using apps (e.g., Khan Academy, LitCharts, or Writing Tutor) to strengthen students' areas of need.

Reflection Questions:

1. What fears or challenges do you face in allowing student reflection to guide instruction?

2. How can you use students' goals to help focus individual student learning?

3. What role do students' learning goals play in your lesson-planning process?

Teaching Students to Self-Assess

This section addresses how you can teach students to use reflection for self-assessment by clarifying standards, scaffolding reflection for beginners using tools like Google Forms, offering students a choice of formats in which to present their reflections, helping students to extend and deepen their reflections, and teaching students to chart their learning progress.

Demystifying the Standards

Before students can assess themselves, they must understand the criteria against which they will be judged. Too often, standards' language is incomprehensible to our kids. Thus, we need to introduce the standards to students in a clear, meaningful way. We must make standards transparent to students at the beginning of every school year and then continually connect learning back to the standards to ensure that students understand what we are looking for.

One way to parse the standards is to break students into groups that each rewrite one of the main standards for the current unit in language they understand. Start the activity by breaking down and rewriting a standard together as a class, applying it to content or skills that students are already familiar with, and then asking students to write a sentence strip with the new rewritten standard to hang on the wall. For example, students may rewrite the standard "Write arguments to support claims in an analysis of substantive topics or texts, using valid reasoning and relevant and sufficient evidence" as "Support claims using appropriate textual evidence in argument papers."

Students need to know which standards each of their assignments or formal assessments addresses. Hang the rewritten versions of the standards on the classroom walls, and refer to them regularly during instruction. Make sure that when it comes time to reflect, students know how well they met the standards that the lesson aligned with.

Consider adding the relevant standards to your assignment sheets, and always allow time to go over what the standards mean. If students don't understand what content or skill the standard addresses, they will be unable to provide evidence showing where they are with regard to that particular standard.

> **Tip:** The more you integrate standards into the learning process, the more transparent the learning purpose and process become. Make sure to have the standards visible with their accompanying learning targets in at least one location in your classroom.

The more knowledgeable students are about the standards, the more readily they will be able to discuss their proficiency against them. When students know the target they are shooting for, they have a much easier time aiming at it and hitting it.

Easing Beginners into Reflection with Google Forms

It is often essential to scaffold the reflection process for beginners. One method I have used successfully is providing students with a premade Google Form listing pointed questions, each one accompanied by a second, less formal question or direction that leads students back to their own work to provide evidence of their learning. Consider the following sample form.

1. Which assignment or unit are you completing this form for? (What did we just finish?)

2. What do you think was the purpose of the assignment or unit? (In your own words, explain why you were asked to do this assignment.)

3. What were you asked to do? (Explain the assignment in your own words.)

4. Do you believe you were able to meet the objectives of the assignment? (Did you learn what you were supposed to learn? Yes / No / Maybe)

5. What have you learned from this assignment? (Be specific.)

6. Which standards do you think the assignment addressed? (Based on the Common Core State Standards or ISTE Standards)

7. Which standards are you meeting or exceeding? (Please copy and paste the standards into the box.)

8. How do you know you are meeting or exceeding these standards? (Please provide evidence from your work.)

9. Which standards do you still need to work on? (Please copy and paste the standards into the box.)

10. How do you know you still need to work on these standards? (Please provide evidence from your work.)

11. Were you given enough time to complete the assignment? (Yes / No)

12. Did you get enough help over the course of this assignment? (Conference help, peer help, teacher help? Yes / No)

13. If you believe you didn't get enough help, did you ask for more? (If no, why not?)

14. What kinds of help are most useful for you? (Teacher help—small group / Teacher help—one-on-one / Peer conference / More time / Modification / Directions and examples provided / Working in groups)

15. Overall, how would you assess yourself on this assignment? (Rate yourself and then discuss what you would do differently in the future.)

Another way to differentiate this form would be to provide a list of the standards that the assignment or unit aligns with and let students check off the standards that they believe they have addressed and the ones they need to continue to work on. Or you could ask specific questions about students' individual learning goals and their completion of those goals. You can adjust the form for different classes or levels of mastery for each grade level as needed.

The answers provided in each form should be the basis of an in-class conference held for each student at the end of a unit before the midterm and at the end of the semester. During these conferences, you use the data provided to see if what you are teaching is actually what is being learned. A useful feature of Google Forms is that each kind of question provides a different kind of data calculation (e.g., multiple-choice questions yield a pie chart in the summary), enabling the teacher to see how the class is doing overall and make on-the-fly decisions to improve learning. Google Forms provides the summary output as a graphic showing the results at a glance and an extended form (see Figure 2 for an example).

In the form shown in Figure 2, each question generates a column and every answer a row. All of the student work is gathered neatly in a spreadsheet that the teacher can return to and annotate as needed once conferences are completed.

It's important to provide students with feedback on their answers, especially the first few times they complete these forms, so that they understand the expectation for the answers to the questionnaire. It is also a good idea to show them samples of what good answers to the questions look like. If you have students fill in these forms regularly, they will become accustomed to answering the questions fully and appropriately and will feel more comfortable with standards.

FIGURE 2: **Extended Google Form**

Which assignment or unit are you completing this form for?	What do you feel was the purpose of the assignment/unit?	What were you asked to do?	Do you feel you were able to meet the objectives of the assignment?	What have you learned from this assignment?
A partner profile piece	My class was asked to complete this assignment because Ms. Sackstein thought it was a good idea for students to get to know each other mixed in with some of the newer kids who attend at WJPS.	My class was asked to conduct an interview with a random person of Ms. Sackstein's choosing between the new kids and the kids who have been there for years. Then we would have to sit down and ask open-ended questions that will explain the back story and the reason why they wanted to come to WJPS in high school. And after we collected as much information as possible, we would gather all our notes to e-mail our teacher for grading.	yes	I learned that everyone has their own different opinion, my partner that I interviewed. I found out that any of the questions I asked weren't the answers I was looking for.
Interview	I think the purpose of the assignment was to get to know our classmates better.	We had to interview our partner for the assignment and ask questions and put the information we got in words.	yes	I learned how to take interviews.
An interview and an article based on that interview.	To gain important skills on how to interview and how to write an interview based on those standards.	We had to interview a fellow student and then write an article about that student.	maybe	I learned how to interview someone, and write an article based on that interview.

Offering a Choice of Reflection Formats

Students' next step in using reflection for self-assessment is to transform their answers to the reflection prompts into thought-out narrative pieces. Students can opt to create a written or spoken reflection. Whether it's in writing, delivered in a one-on-one conference, or through a video, the reflection will provide essential information about the student that can help you better assess his or her learning.

It is important to make sure students know that reflection is about the learning and the discussion, not necessarily the format. If you have a student who is not completing the reflection because she hates to write, ask her if she would rather reflect via a voice memo, a message through Voxer, or a short video.

> **Tip:** Let students know that they have options for how they present their reflections to you or to others. The more ownership students feel over their reflections, the more useful the reflections will be to their learning.

Each format provides a different kind of depth. If a student chooses to write, the teacher will gain insight into his or her strengths and weaknesses as a writer. If a student chooses to speak on an audio file, the teacher can gauge the student's confidence through his or her vocal inflections, pauses, and pace. Auditory messages can be extremely powerful and generate fruitful discussion even when the participants aren't in the same place.

⚡ **Tip:** Voxer is a great app that acts as a walkie-talkie. Students can talk to teachers and vice versa, not just for reflection but also for formative feedback throughout the learning process.

Video is another avenue for student reflection. This format includes all the features of the audio format while also providing the benefit of seeing the student's facial expressions and physical mannerisms, which can strongly indicate how a student feels about his or her learning.

Finally, if a student has communication challenges, consider allowing him or her to draw a reflection. This can segue into a fuller conversation and provide an entry point for the student to discuss what he or she drew and why.

We must home in on the details our students give us in their reflections, learn from that information, and adjust our teaching accordingly. Regardless of how students decide to reflect, the process will enrich their lives, and reflection will become an important adult skill that will support them in their careers and relationships.

Deepening Students' Reflections

The first reflection you receive from your students will likely be exceedingly short and address how much or how little they enjoyed the assignment. Of course, this is not the purpose of reflection, as you should remind them.

Figure 3 depicts a reflection poster I created that hangs in every classroom in my school as a reminder. If every teacher in a learning community hangs this poster in his or her classroom and holds similar expectations for student reflections, then students will get plenty of practice writing them, which will in turn deepen their overall learning.

FIGURE 3: How Do I Reflect?

What should your reflection include?
— Restate in your own words what the assignment asked you to do.
— Discuss your process for completion.
— Address standards appropriate to the assignment AND how you met them using evidence from your work.

Consider:
— What did you learn?
— How did you overcome challenges?
— What would you do differently next time?
— How would you assess yourself?

What should your reflection look like?
— An essay (do not just answer the above questions), at least one full page with multiple paragraphs, single-spaced.

What should your reflection NOT look like?
— Bad habits of other group members (focus on yourself).
— Whether or not you liked an assignment (unless there is constructive feedback as well).
— Just answers to the above questions without a narrative.

One way to get students to make the leap to deeper, more thoughtful reflection is to walk the whole class through the steps of writing a reflection at the end of a unit or a specific assignment. First, tell students to explain what the task asked them to do in their own words, and give them an appropriate amount of time—say, five minutes—to write that initial paragraph. Circulate through the room, providing feedback to students as needed. Because there will always be students looking to accomplish the bare minimum, ask clarifying questions that prompt students to extend their responses (e.g., "You said that you had to write an article; can you explain what kind of article you had to write and what needed to be included in it?").

Here is the introductory paragraph from the reflection of a 9th grade English language learner with an individualized education program. Note that in a few short sentences, this student is able to articulate the exact requirements of the assignment:

> For this assignment, we were asked to pick a situation recently on the news. After picking the situation, we had to write about the situation in our local area by putting quotes from the people in the area about their thoughts. We needed at least three quotes from three different people on their thoughts/responses. Also, it was mandatory to cite where we got our information from in our news article.

Next, deliver the second prompt: "Write a second paragraph discussing the process you used to complete the assignment." Remind students to be thorough, considering the steps they took and the specific learning they achieved.

Here is the second paragraph from the same 9th grade student's reflection:

To complete this assignment, I wrote out my first draft with no quotes. After writing it out, I started to fill in some quotes to where they should belong to make them fit with the information on our situation to make it local news. Then, I went back and edited my organization and headline because those are my weakest things I wanted to focus on to improve. I made sure my information was listed from most important to least important. Also, to have a strong active headline, I wrote out three different headlines and chose the best one.

Coaching students through these initial steps helps them start to understand the qualities that you are looking for. It's also useful to provide samples of both high-level and low-level reflections for students to examine. You may want to have them review a sample reflection against the criteria the teacher has given them (as shown in Figure 3) and note how the reflection met or failed to meet those expectations and dissect the document's strengths and weaknesses as a class.

Tip: Generally, share only work samples that are within students' range of skill. Don't show samples from a 12th grade AP class to a lower-track 9th grade class. Seeing the work of more advanced kids can be discouraging and demotivating. That doesn't mean that students who are ready for the challenge shouldn't see higher-level samples; the key is to provide students with just enough challenge to propel them forward.

The most difficult part of deepening reflection is also the part that's most essential to student self-assessment: having students use evidence from their work to show how well they have met the standards. Teaching students to do this takes time. I tell my students to imagine that they're writing an argument paper in which they must prove their point, where meeting the standards is their point and their work is the proof.

Providing students with the specific standards they are supposed to meet can get them on the right track the first couple of times they write reflections. Higher-level students who are already familiar with the standards can select the standards that they believe their work did the best job of meeting. Walk students through the first standard and ask them to assess whether they are approaching, meeting, or exceeding it, and to provide evidence from their work to support their assertion.

The following sample, which describes how the student changed her headline to incorporate active words, uses language from the rubric provided to ensure a deeper connection to her learning.

> I've exceeded the standards. I've had trouble on having an active engaging headline. In my news article's headline, **Ebola puts an end to Doctor's life**, the word "puts" is my active verb. Also, I've exceeded the standards of sentence structure to make the news article stronger rather than weakening it. For example, in my news article I stated the information

from most important to least important to keep readers engaged.

> I've learned that a journalist can not include any opinion whatsoever, only if it is quotes by someone. Also, quoting from people makes it more of a local news story to make it more engaging for people to be more interested in what's happening around them.

For the final prompt, ask students to describe any challenges they faced, how they tackled those problems, and what they would do differently in the future. This is the time for students to discuss their learning: what did they actually learn? How do they know? Do they believe that they are proficient now?

Here is the concluding paragraph of our 9th grader's reflection:

> I liked this assignment because it gives us a sense of how journalists work. A journalist isn't just writing what they want but there are rules to follow. For example, including false facts can lose your trust as a journalist and a person. I may not want to be a journalist when I'm older but we can see how journalists write with the rules they have to follow. Also, we can see how difficult it is not to include a lot of stuff but it's part of being a journalist.

This paragraph clearly shows what the student has learned and the importance of the assignment. Her whole reflection showed me that she understands the tenets of news writing and will be able to apply this knowledge if she's later asked to write a news story on a different topic.

Providing feedback is essential to students' understanding of what we expect to see in their reflections. We need to continue to remind students of the qualities of strong reflective pieces and provide them with multiple supports and strategies until they find their reflecting voice. Once they get the hang of the process, they—and we—will see a real difference in their learning.

Teaching Students to Chart Their Progress

Isolated reflections at various points during a student's learning are fine, but consider how much more powerful the reflection process would be if it connected all learning as a progression. Teaching students to track their own progress and continually reflect on their growth is essential to their learning and to the teacher's ability to keep tabs on every student's learning.

Imagine this scenario: a student has been told by his science teacher that he needs to generate more detailed hypotheses. He struggled with this the first time, so his teacher gave him some strategies to help him improve his lab reports. For example, she told him to think of his hypothesis in terms of a question he is trying to answer, to write three different versions and settle on the one that works, or to rewrite the hypothesis after he has his findings. For his next lab write-up, the student refers to the last round of feedback and strategies, which he has been tracking in a notebook or a Google Doc, and notes in the Google Doc which feedback or strategies he has applied.

Because the student has taken the time to illuminate what he has been working on, the teacher knows which areas need further feedback. By following this process with the whole class, the teacher will be able to focus on the specific skills each student is working on.

> **Tip:** Read students' reflections before reading their work to get a sense of how well they think they did. Note what each student struggled with so that the feedback you give to students will be more targeted and meaningful.

Early in the year, set a routine that makes clear to students that they are expected to document the feedback they receive. How you do this may vary depending on the age and mastery level of your students. Every student should either designate an area in his or her notebook specifically for feedback and observations or maintain a running Google Doc that records the date, the assignment, the specific feedback, the person who provided the feedback, and a section for revised work that has incorporated the feedback provided. The final reflective piece draws from this documentation. Figure 4 depicts an example of how this might look in Google Docs.

Students must form the habit of returning to these notes to adjust goals, demonstrate progress, and request support in areas of particular challenge. When students keep

FIGURE 4: **Sample Student Documentation of Feedback and Progress**

Assignment and date	Feedback provided	Strategy or action taken	Feedback after strategy applied	Questions	Goals	Mastery reached?
3/21—sample assignment	need to develop context in my opening paragraph to better engage the reader	considered my thesis statement and how it more broadly connected with the reader as per my conversation with the teacher	I was able to create some context, but I didn't go far enough. This time I only gave a sentence and it felt tagged on. Getting closer, but need to add more to transition smoothly	How do I know which part of my thesis determines the best context?	Develop a strong introductory paragraph in my next paper that employs 3–4 sentences of context and then smoothly transition into a clear thesis statement	still working on it—approaching standards still

this documentation, their ability to ask for thoughtful, targeted feedback and assistance improves—and so does their learning.

Reflection Questions:

1. How do you introduce standards to students?

2. How might you make the standards a part of the learning in your classes?

3. How can you teach the standards to students at varying mastery levels to make the most meaning out of them?

4. Why must students understand the criteria for learning before they start?

5. How can you make the criteria for success evident to students?

6. Who tracks learning in your space? Why? How? Jot down some ways in which you might adjust your current practices, if necessary.

Making Time to Reflect

To get good at anything, students must have time to engage in reflection and self-assessment. It's not enough to ask them to do it on their own; we must allot class time for these important practices. If we make reflection feel like an afterthought, then students will never understand its necessity or value.

This section addresses ways to incorporate reflection into class time and when and how often to use reflection.

Tip: What we devote time to in class shows what we value, so make time to build a culture of reflection. Nurture the process; don't rush through it.

When and How Often to Reflect in Class

Reflection isn't something done only at the end of an assignment or a unit; there are many times when it's appropriate. For example, we can generate reflections at the beginning of a unit to ascertain students' prior knowledge and set goals.

Scheduling reflection time at the end of each class is an especially effective way to foster a culture of reflection. In lieu of exit tickets, have students keep reflective journals that discuss some element of each day's learning. You can spot-check these journals regularly or as needed, but this shouldn't add much to your already-heavy load. Ask students to reflect every day, answering questions like "What did you learn today?" and "What do you still have questions about?" These journals provide a forum for students to internalize even small pieces of learning and activate connections between different lessons throughout a unit.

Another logical time for both students and teachers to reflect is at the end of the semester or school year, when they can write summative evaluations of the larger learning journey. Where did they start and end? What bumps did they experience along the way? What were their most memorable moments? Their least memorable moments? When you reflect along with your students, voila: you have an opportunity for celebration.

Ultimately, we want students to become thoughtful lifelong learners who don't need to be reminded to reflect on the events of their lives. By following the steps that lead from observation to practice to development to mastery, we eventually develop an acute awareness of who we are and who we want to become.

Replacing Teacher-Centered Grading with Student Self-Assessment

In a world where grades communicate less and less of what an educator needs them to, student reflection and self-assessment can provide the necessary bridge to making that communication more meaningful. If students can articulate which standards they are approaching, meeting, and exceeding and can provide evidence from their work to support their assertions, then why shouldn't they be the final arbiters of their level of mastery?

For too long, educators have allowed nonacademic factors to affect measures of student achievement, diluting the true meaning of whatever letter grades students receive. If learning is truly about achievement, and if reflection aims to help students articulate their own achievement, then maybe it's time to teach students to assess their own level of attainment.

Forms can be used not only as a reflection tool for students but also as a way to gather data on student learning over the course of a marking period. At the end of the period, hold individual meetings with students in which they articulate how well they've met the standards, provide evidence from their work, and assess themselves on their level of mastery accordingly. Done properly, the result will be a more accurate reflection of student learning than a grade based on a point system that prizes compliance and playing the game of school over authentic educational attainment.

This idea may seem far out, but it is actually grounded in common sense. Shouldn't students have some say in the way they're going to be labeled?

Reflecting Regularly Through Blogs or Journals

Regular, ongoing reflection is the gold standard, and a blog is an excellent space for collecting students' insights on their learning. I suggest having students post reflections at least once a week. Because all reflections are kept in one place, students and teachers alike can easily navigate through the blog to track student growth, which sometimes happens so slowly in real time that it's difficult to see.

You can model the blogging process to students by maintaining one of your own to reflect on your class's learning and to connect with an audience of educators. The power of this format is undeniable, which is why it seems selfish not to engage students in it.

The first step is to figure out the best platform (I suggest Kidblog for young students or Blogger for older ones) and then create a community of bloggers in the classroom. Teach students to make their thoughts public, how to appropriately respond to their peers, and how reflection can be communal as well as personal. Students are developing digital citizenship skills and learning not only from the thoughts and ideas in their own heads, but also from points their classmates make that they hadn't even considered. The additional perspective of an audience and the power of connection can only enhance this learning in a new dimension.

If you or your students prefer not to post reflections on a public platform, consider having students keep personal reflection notebooks or maintaining a folder in Google Drive where you collect students' reflections. (Make sure students name the documents appropriately with the title of the assignment they're associated with; no one wants to read 20 reflections named "Untitled"!) Both students and teachers can glean insights from these privacy-controlled formats the same way they would from a blog. Over time, once students build up more confidence, they may be willing to move to a public venue.

Reflection Questions:

1. What message do you send with how you currently schedule reflection or self-assessment in your classes?

2. When is the best time to reflect in your classroom?

3. How often do you invite your students to reflect?

4. How do you differentiate reflection experiences for your students?

5. What have you learned that may lead you to reconsider or make a change in your current class reflection process?

6. What new practice will you implement right away in your classes?

Using Data from Reflection to Assess for Learning

This section addresses how you can glean information from students' reflections to provide formative assessment, develop targeted learning plans, and determine students' mastery.

Generating Individualized Plans for Student Growth

Once students have been taught to carefully examine and reflect on their learning, you can help them create a plan to work toward mastery. Because every student is different, we must determine our best course of action based on what we learn from students and what we know about our content.

Too often, our lessons stem from *our* need to cover content rather than *students'* need to learn. It's time for us to truly listen to what students are saying and adjust our instruction accordingly. Student reflection and self-assessment make this task infinitely simpler.

Let's look at the reflection of a 12th grade student in an elective class. Consider her learning process and discussion of standards. In which areas can she improve? What feedback would you give her?

For this part of the yearlong project we had to make a social media campaign for our company. We had to use Facebook, Twitter, Instagram, Pinterest, or any other social media website we'd like to use and find ways to promote our company. We could use videos, pictures, quizzes, hashtags, etc. to get our company more well known. For my group, we used a quiz to tell customers what smoothie they would be/like from Jamba Juice. I thought this would be a great way to attract customers to try whatever smoothie they are to see if they actually like it. This starts a chain reaction because they'll tell their friends to try it and the quiz will spread. We chose to use both Instagram and Twitter. We used Instagram to advertise smoothie types, where to find coupons, commercials and any other specials we were having. We used Twitter as a place to give promotions to followers and people could use the hashtag "#myjamba" to tweet the outcome of the quiz and random quiz takers were given a free smoothie.

I feel we met all standards for this portion of the project. We met **1. Creativity and innovation** (a. Apply existing knowledge to generate new ideas, products, or processes, b. Create original works as a means of personal or group expression, d. Identify trends and forecast possibilities). For this part of the project we had to be very creative in order to have an effective campaign. We met this standard when creating the quiz that linked both the Twitter and Instagram together. **2. Communication and collaboration** (a. Interact, collaborate, and publish with peers, experts, or others employing a variety of digital environments and media, b. Communicate information and ideas effectively to multiple audiences using a variety of media and for-mats, d. Contribute to project teams to produce original works or solve problems). We actually collaborated with another group, we asked a Target group if they wanted to help promote each other. Both groups benefited from this because we have similar but slightly different target groups. **3. Research and information fluency** (a. Plan strategies to guide inquiry, b. Locate, organize, ana-lyze, evaluate, synthesize, and ethically use information from a variety of sources and media, d. Process data and report results). Before starting the campaign we looked at what would be best for us to use (Twitter, Facebook, etc.) and found that Twitter and Instagram would be best for us. **4. Critical thinking, problem solving, and decision making** (a. Identify and define authentic prob-lems and significant questions for investigation, b. Plan and manage activities to develop a solution or complete a project). **5. Digital citizenship** (a. Advocate and prac-tice safe, legal, and responsible use of information and technology, b. Exhibit a positive attitude toward using technology that supports collaboration, learning, and productivity, c. Demonstrate personal responsibility for lifelong learning, d. Exhibit leadership for digital citizenship). We practiced safe and legal use of technology by making our accounts private and writing in the bio that Jamba Juice should not be held responsible for anything we said on Twitter or Instagram. **6. Technology operations and concepts** (a. Understand and use technology systems, b. Select and use applications effectively and productively, d. Transfer current knowledge to learning of new technologies). We knew how to use Twitter and Instagram the way it should be used and learned more about hashtags and how to limit what we say per tweet in order to get everything out we wanted to say.

I thought that out of all the parts of the projects we've done this is one of the most useful. We all use Facebook, Twitter, Instagram, Pinterest, and more on a daily basis and this gave us a new way to use it. If we were ever to need to promote ourselves or a product we now know what to do and how to go about it in order to be effective.

The process is clearly written, and the narrative is easy to follow. This student clearly understands why we reflect. My biggest piece of feedback would be that the student did not provide enough evidence from the group's work to show that she met the standards as she claims. There is an awareness of the connection, but not a depth of understanding.

Now consider the following reflection from a 12th grade AP student. What strengths does this student exhibit? What can she help other students with? What challenges does she discuss, and what strategies might she use to overcome these challenges?

For this assignment, students had to select a prompt from a list from the sheet to write an analysis paper that answers the task. I decided to use two of the questions: Compare the character of Gatsby to that of Tom. How are the two men similar and different? How are East Egg and West Egg different from each other? What makes East Egg more appealing than West Egg and why? Combining both of these prompts, I was able to use the setting (West and East Eggs) to characterize the people in the book.

I started off this paper by doing an outline and because I had the actual text, it was much easier to annotate and mark the strategies Fitzgerald used in his novel. Here, I've met College Board standard R4.2.2, "Marks and annotates texts and takes notes during or after reading to identify and elaborate key ideas" [The College Board, 2006]. As I was reading, I took notes of different strategies and evidence I can use that demonstrates the correlation between the elements. I felt that this book was easy to understand and straightforward which made it a little easier to write the essay. However, the most difficult part was deciding what exactly I want to write about, and what to analyze. There was so much going on in the novel and it was hard to choose what to include and what not to include. Once I figured out what I planned on writing, my essay turned out to be much longer than expected. The easiest part of this assignment was of course, finding the quotes. I met standard CCSS.ELA-LITERACY.RL. 11-12.1, "Cite strong and thorough textual evidence to support analysis of what the text says explicitly as well as inferences drawn from the text, including determining where the text leaves matters uncertain" [National Governors Association Center for Best Practices & Council of Chief State School Officers, 2010]. There was much written about Tom and Gatsby that clearly supported each of my arguments. Fitzgerald made it very clear how different Tom and Gatsby are on the surface, so finding good text evidence was pretty simple.

From here on, I created a rough first draft. It was definitely very unorganized and hard to understand because sometimes I would skip ahead two body paragraphs to write a fourth one, or go back and write the conclusion. My thoughts were unorganized and usually, midway through writing, I would think of a new idea and add that in with the rest of my essay. Although I did create a basic outline, next time I think that I shouldn't be going back and forth because on the real AP exam, I wouldn't have enough time to do so. My peers and Ms. Sackstein helped me a lot throughout the process because they gave me really good feedback. This challenged me to work harder on my paper. So I began to work on my second draft by expanding my supporting paragraphs with comparisons of Gatsby and Tom and their social class.

Another challenge I've faced was writing the introduction of my essay. Unlike my other analysis papers, I wrote too much in the introduction and gave everything away. So I had to cut back and revise a couple of times. It was important for me to introduce the topic and elements without overwhelming the readers with too much information. My main focus of the paper was to analyze the differences between Tom and Gatsby. Here, I met CCSS.ELA-LITERACY.RL.11-12.5 where I had to analyze how an author's choices concerning how to structure specific parts of a text (e.g., the choice of where to begin or end a story, the choice to provide a comedic or tragic resolution) contribute to its overall structure and meaning as well as its aesthetic impact.

It took me a while to get my ideas and thoughts more structured and concise. This was definitely not an easy assignment for me. My essay was revised multiple times throughout this whole process so I can deliver an understandable interpretation of Fitzgerald's work.

I met College Board standard W5.1 ("Student edits for conventions of standard written English and usage") and W5.2 ("Student employs proofreading strategies and consults resources to correct errors in spelling, capitalization, and punctuation") [The College Board, 2006]. My main concern is that there's so much going on in my paper that it can confuse the readers. Hopefully, that's not the case but I really tried my hardest to compare the character and the setting of the novel.

Did you notice how artfully this student took us through her writing process and learning? She noted measurable evidence, included standards to demonstrate her achievement and mastery, and exuded a strong sense of self.

At the beginning of the year, reflections aren't this comprehensive or polished, but by March, my seniors have usually internalized the process and are capable of producing thoughtful, sophisticated reflective pieces that demonstrate their metacognitive abilities and propel their learning process forward. As they move on to college, they feel confident that their ability to reflect deeply will serve them well.

Determining Mastery

What does mastery look like? Ask five different educators, and you'll get five different answers. One of the biggest challenges of teaching is that so much of it is subjective.

Although we try to make it objective so that we can assess it appropriately, it's difficult to truly quantify students' learning.

Still, this much we can probably agree on: a student has achieved mastery when he or she can consistently demonstrate proficiency in a particular task, skill, or set of content and is capable of teaching it to a peer. It's not good enough for a student to hit the mark once; that could just be a lucky chance. If a student can reproduce the same successful outcome in a number of tasks in different settings, however, then it is fair to say that mastery has been achieved.

Consider this scenario: algebraic equations are taught early in the year, and most students struggle with the process of solving the equations. It's new and foreign, and it takes time to develop a level of familiarity. So teachers offer multiple opportunities for students to practice the equations by giving them a series of different algebraic equations to solve. Some students get it relatively quickly, while others need more practice.

Over time, it is evident that the students who have reached proficiency have succeeded because all of the various tasks they have been doing mimic the original task. True mastery comes when you can present students with a new challenge that they have never seen, and they know how to apply their skills and knowledge to meet the challenge every time. In the case of algebraic equations, this might be in the context of authentic problem-based learning, when students aren't just given a straightforward problem to solve but must identify the problem themselves.

This is called transfer of learning, and it's the key skill we want to instill in our students.

Students need to be able to transfer the knowledge, skills, and content we teach them to other areas of their lives. One of the major challenges in getting buy-in from students is that they don't understand how what we teach them applies to their own lives. Mastery comes when students can identify a challenge in any area of their lives and know how to reach the best solution. They can tackle the challenge and see it through, and then they can talk about why they made the choices they did. The reflective cycle continues long after the initial lesson has been taught.

Reflection Questions:

1. How do you empower students to track their own progress?

2. In what ways do you adjust learning to suit each student's needs?

3. What does mastery look like to you? Do your students know? How do you communicate that with them?

4. Who determines mastery?

To give your feedback on this publication and
be entered into a drawing for a free ASCD
Arias e-book, please visit
www.ascd.org/ariasfeedback

ENCORE

Sample Student Reflections

Sample 1: Hamlet

For this assignment, we were able to choose our own groups and then were assigned a scene from either Act 4 or Act 5. Because there were four people in our group (Laina, DaHae, Michelle, and I) we were given one of the longer scenes, Act 5 Scene 2, which is also the last scene.

As part of the assignment, my group members and I had to create a comic strip that summarized the important parts of the scene. We chose to have six of the major events and condensed everything else into those six events. Then we used quotes that paraphrased/summarized what that event talked about. Finally, in the screencast, we analyzed the scene and each cell overall.

To try to make the work spread evenly, we split up the six events between the four of us. I was chosen to read, summarize, and analyze the beginning part of the scene where Hamlet tells Horatio about him almost being executed on orders by the King and later where Osric asks Hamlet to fight Laertes. One way that I analyzed the two cells was trying to connect ideas or plots to the rest of the play. (Analyze a complex set of ideas or sequence of events and explain how specific individuals, ideas, or events interact and develop over the course of the text.)

For example, we see in previous acts how the King tried to have Hamlet killed and in Act 5 Scene 2 we see the results of that plan. Hamlet wasn't killed because he switched the letters. This allowed for Hamlet to have a more personal and stronger revenge. It also shows how serious the King was in trying to set up Hamlet, instead of letting Hamlet live in England, he was sent to be executed there.

This analysis was a little more difficult than I anticipated it to be. As I've said in previous reflections, Shakespearean language is hard so by me going back to reread the scene after the initial perusal, I was able to read the scene slowly and comprehend what Shakespeare wanted to say. Of course, I didn't get everything because I can't understand him that well, but I thought that I was able to touch upon several of the ideas that I believed were important.

During the analysis, all my group members looked through the analysis to make sure that we wrote down what we believed was central to the scene. By doing so, I noticed that there were several obvious and maybe not so obvious themes that sort of come into play during the last scene of the play. (Determine two or more central ideas of a text and analyze their development over the course of the text, including how they interact and build on one another to provide a complex analysis; provide an objective summary of the text.) For example, the most obvious theme, Revenge, shows that even though we want to take revenge on somebody for what they had done to us or someone else, that revenge will lead to harm being done to innocent bystanders and even ourselves. Shakespeare shows that through Hamlet, revenge is pointless because it will never help us, it will only harm us. Shakespeare also touches upon the idea of something completely consuming us. He shows that we should never get so caught up into one idea that we forget about everything else.

I believe overall that the project went okay. I wish that we could have had a little longer (maybe a day or two) so that my whole group could sit together and go over each analysis one by one to refine them and expand upon other points. Because some of my group members were absent on different days, there was never really any good day or time to get together and work. Even though we got together on the weekend and after school, there were still people absent. It created more difficulties for us as a group.

The comic strip was relatively easier than anything else we've had to do. Because we had predetermined the events we would use, the biggest problems we had were trying to find out what quotes we should use. In the end, we just paraphrased and summarized what the characters said, condensing them into a couple lines that they could say.

Overall, I will be happy to never have to do a screen-cast again. These things are hard, especially with a book that I can't really understand!

Sample 2: Photojournalism

For this assignment we were asked to document our days at school for a week—in classes, in the hallways, at lunch, etc. I mostly did the halls and a specific classroom. We had to document every aspect of our day and make sure that we took our best photos because it is the last project of photojournalism. We had time in class to plan, and take pictures, but we needed permission. After we select 5–7 photos that we took, and describe why we decided to take the picture, but not what's in it.

For completion, I started on a Monday to take a picture each day. I decided to angle them in a specific way, so it would seem more interesting. While I gathered my photos, I used a few rules and made the compositions stand out. After that I put them on a doc and used my knowledge of what I know about photojournalism to describe the specific compositions of the photos such as the lighting, angles, contrast, and simplicity.

I was able to understand how to conduct short as well as more sustained research projects based on focused questions, demonstrating understanding of the subject under investigation. I used my notes for more understanding of the composition, and actually tried to take good-quality photos. Also, I was able to gather the relevant information from multiple print and digital sources (once again from my notes and the links that were sent to me), assess the credibility and accuracy of each source, and integrate the information while avoiding plagiarism.

I had difficulty with capturing the photos in certain compositions. I do admit that I am not good at taking photos. It was hard to select and use applications effectively and productively, as well. Positioning the camera was difficult, and before pressing the camera button I wanted to be able to see the shape that the photo is in, and if later on I would have to add adjustments.

When there is a next time, I want to be an expert toward this project and be more creative with the photos and compositions. Such shape, and objects in the photos can have a meaning—even if it is a little bit of it. It would be fun going around, and taking pictures with a professional camera while still learning about photography.

Additional Resources

- **Sample assessment form template:** https://docs.google.com/forms/d/16QvBXz6xsnPivW9tQuPMAjATYzdCiKF_EbdxAHtVzdQ/viewform?c=0&w=1

- **Screencast on using Google Forms to gather student data:** https://www.youtube.com/watch?v=0Dkr3hHrevg&feature=youtu.be

- **Screencast on using Google Forms to prepare for student conferences:** https://www.youtube.com/watch?v=335NugJYazo&feature=youtu.be

- **Screencast examining standards-based student reflection samples:** https://www.youtube.com/watch?v=9MlN4YGIfT8&feature=youtu.be

- **WizIQ webinar on reflection:** https://www.wiziq.com/course/96127-teaching-students-to-reflect-on-personal-learning

- **Blog post on intentional classrooms:** http://starrsackstein.com/category/intentional-classrooms

- **Blog post on student conferences:** http://starrsackstein.com/category/class-time-conferences-for-individualized-feedback-and-plans

- **Blog post on how Google Docs enhances feedback:** http://starrsackstein.com/category/hours-gone-by-but-ill-never-stop-google-docs-improve-the-feedback-experience

- **Blog post on recognizing progress:** http://starrsackstein.com/category/seeing-and-recognizing-progress

References

The College Board. (2006). *College Board Standards for college success: English language arts*. New York: Author. Retrieved from http://www.collegeboard.com/prod_downloads/about/association/academic/english-language-arts_cbscs.pdf

National Governors Association Center for Best Practices (NGA Center) & Council of Chief State School Officers (CCSSO). (2010). *Common Core State Standards for English language arts & literacy in history/social studies, science, and technical subjects*. Washington, DC: Author. Retrieved from http://www.corestandards.org/ELA-Literacy

Related ASCD Resources

At the time of publication, the following ASCD resources were available (ASCD stock numbers appear in parentheses). For up-to-date information about ASCD resources, go to www.ascd.org.

ASCD EDge® Group
Exchange ideas and connect with other educators interested in assessment and 21st century learning on the social networking site ASCD EDge at edge.ascd.org.

Print Products
Digital Learning Strategies: How Do I Assign and Assess 21st Century Work? (ASCD Arias) by Michael Fisher (#SF114045)
Grading Smarter, Not Harder: Assessment Strategies That Motivate Kids and Help Them Learn by Myron Dueck (#114003)
How to Design Questions and Tasks to Assess Student Thinking by Susan M. Brookhart (#114014)
Rethinking Grading: Meaningful Assessment for Standards-Based Learning by Cathy Vatterott (#115001)

DVDs
Assessment for 21st Century Learning DVD Set (#610010)
How to Informally Assess Student Learning (#605121)

ASCD PD Online© Courses
Formative Assessment: Deepening Understanding (#PD11OC101M)
The Reflective Educator (#PD11OC114M)
Technology in Schools: A Balanced Perspective (#PD11OC109M)

For more information: send e-mail to member@ascd.org; call 1-800-933-2723 or 703-578-9600, press 2; send a fax to 703-575-5400; or write to Information Services, ASCD, 1703 N. Beauregard St., Alexandria, VA 22311-1714 USA.

About the Author

 Starr Sackstein is an English and journalism teacher at World Journalism Preparatory School in Flushing, New York, where she has thrown out grades in favor of developing students' ability to articulate their own growth. She also directs students in running a multimedia news outlet at WJPSnews.com.

A veteran educator, she started her career at Far Rockaway High School in New York more than 13 years ago. She was honored by the Dow Jones News Fund as a Special Recognition Adviser in 2011 and named an Outstanding Educator of the Year by *Education Update* in 2012.

She earned National Board Certification in 2013 and is a certified Master Journalism Educator through the Journalism Education Association (JEA). She serves as the New York State Director to JEA to help advisers in New York better grow journalism programs.

She is the author of *Teaching Mythology Exposed*: *Helping Teachers Create Visionary Classroom Perspective* (2014) and *Blogging for Educators: Writing for Professional Learning* (2015). She writes for *Education Week Teacher*'s blog *Work in Progress* in addition to maintaining her personal blog (StarrSackstein.com), where she discusses education reform and all aspects of being a teacher. She co-moderates

#sunchat and contributes to #NYedChat on Twitter. She has made the Bammy Awards finals for Secondary High School Educator in 2014 and for Educational Commentator/Blogger in 2015. In speaking engagements, she talks about blogging, journalism education, throwing out grades and BYOD, and helping people see that technology doesn't have to be feared.

She balances her busy career of writing and teaching with being the mom to 10-year-old Logan. Seeing the world through his eyes reminds her why education needs to change for every child.

She can be reached at mssackstein@gmail.com, as well as through Twitter (@MsSackstein) and Facebook (https://www.facebook.com/pages/Starr-Sackstein-MJE/173509889399007).